LOOSE LEAVES FROM MY BIBLE

LOOSE LEAVES FROM MY BIBLE

SOME PARAPHRASES BY

David Pawson

Anchor Recordings

First published 1994
This edition published in Great Britain 2014
by
Anchor Recordings Ltd
72 The Street
Kennington
Ashford
TN24 9HS

For more of David Pawson's teaching,
including MP3s, DVDs and CDs, go to
www.davidpawson.com
For further information, email: info@davidpawsonministry.com

ISBN 978-1-909886-55-1

Printed by Lightning Source

Contents

INTRODUCTION

I have been teaching others the Bible for over forty years. To my astonishment, tape recordings of these studies in God's word have been distributed by the thousand to over a hundred countries. Now I am making videos, under the general title: "Unlocking the Old and New Testaments", which look like having a similar appeal.

One problem has been which version to use. We are blessed with so many, perhaps too many, English translations. I never used the Authorised (King James) Version; its quaint vocabulary and phraseology were already past their sell-by date when I launched into preaching. I began with the Revised Standard Version, then "just out"; it stood me in good stead for some years. Then Today's English Version (or Good News Bible) appeared. In my desire to communicate the truth in up-to-date terms, I used it for a few years; but it quickly lost its freshness for me and, I sensed, for my listeners. I am now wedded to the New International Version (devotees interpret N.I.V. as "Nearly Infallible Version"!). It is by far the easiest to read aloud with real meaning.

Occasionally, I have been dissatisfied with all the available versions (I have over thirty). Then I have produced my own! It has usually been more of a paraphrase than a translation, aiming to bring out the subtle nuances of the original text. They have created considerable interest and copies have been requested. This booklet contains a selection of the most popular, together with notes about their origin.

The reason for doing it has varied. Sometimes I have felt that the usual wording is too familiar and no longer attracts attention or stimulates a response (Genesis 1, Psalm 23 and John 1 are classic examples). In other cases, the exact opposite applies; the passage is so unfamiliar that it appears unreal or irrelevant.

The reason for tackling Paul's letter to the Galatians was neither of these, but the need for a version that would communicate his intellectual argument, moral appeal and emotional anger more effectively. The reader can judge whether I have succeeded.

Most modern Bibles print prose and poetry differently. The distinction is important. When God wants us to understand his thoughts, he inspires prose. When he wants us to share his feelings, he uses poetry. Significantly, both praise and prophecy are usually in poetic form, engaging as they do the hearts of man and the heart of God. The usage of poetry in Genesis 1-3 is particularly eloquent, though I trust my rather naïve equivalents will be forgiven.

What should I call "my very own" scripture? Perhaps: "The New Amplified Revised Living Non-standard English Bible"! Or even: "The New King David"! Maybe just simply: "The Colloquial English

Version". That is what it is meant to be – and that will prevent it being translated into any other language. Colloquialisms (like "going the whole hog") are notorious traps for interpreters.

The passages were intended to be read (or sung) aloud. The form of words was carefully chosen to render the common pulpit monotone impossible. Tone of voice can convey the meaning very effectively. Readers are invited to try reading the texts to someone else.

I prepared these extracts for others, but I was greatly blessed myself. Somehow, as I put God's word into my words, it became part of me in a fresh way. I felt like Jeremiah and Ezekiel, who ate their message (Jeremiah 15:16; Ezekiel 3:2).

So here is one reader's digest of the Book of books. If you get half the delight in the reading as I did in the writing, it will have been worth it.

May the Lord speak to you afresh!

David Pawson
Sherborne St John, 1994

THE WEEK IT ALL WENT RIGHT AND THE DAY IT ALL WENT WRONG
(Genesis 1 – 3)

Introduction

If the Bible is about the drama of redemption, the first few pages outline the stage, the cast and the plot. Without these, the rest would be incomprehensible. In particular, the very last pages would lose much of their significance.

We have here God's explanation why we live in such a wonderful world and why it is in such a mess – how good things went bad.

Of course, no-one can improve on the language of Genesis 1. It bears all the hallmarks of direct composition by a divine mind and is probably one of the few passages of scripture without any trace of the human writer. To analyse it is to dissect a flower; knowledge is gained, but beauty is lost.

Nevertheless, the traditional translation may be so well known that the sheer wonder of it is diminished. The sense of God's power, his orderly and imaginative mind, his sheer pleasure, his desire to bless as well as create, his leisure as well as his work – all this and more can escape us through over-familiarity.

This paraphrase has stimulated interest whenever I have used it. Perhaps it was born when, after our little daughter had listened to this chapter being read, she thought for a moment and then observed: "No sooner said than done!" It was a perfect summary.

One problem arises from chapter 2 onwards. God now has a name (as has man). It is composed of four Hebrew letters: JHVH (pronounced 'Yahweh', not 'Jehovah'). Derived from the verb "to be", it can be variously translated – am, being, etc. The customary habit of English translators has been to use "LORD" (in capital letters), but this is quite a different word (in Hebrew: "Adonai").

I prayed about this and asked the Lord to give me an English word that would give me an emotional as well as an intellectual understanding of his name. Immediately, the word "always" came into my mind, so I have used this. God has many "second" names that go with it – Always-my-helper, Always-my-provider, Always-my-healer and so on.

One of Jesus' two hundred and fifty names and titles is "Yes", (2 Corinthians 1:20). With a Father called "Always" and a Son called "Yes", we could hardly have a more positive faith! And we need to remember that the Son was one of the "us" at creation, together with God and the Spirit.

It is striking that the word for 'God' is plural. Strictly speaking, the Hebrew word "Elohim" is used for three (or more) "gods". Yet the verbs are all singular – a remarkable pointer to our three-in-one God. I could not think of a way to bring out this subtle point in my translation, so simply mention it.

One final matter – where the Hebrew is in poetic form, I have indicated this with English rhyme (apologies to Moses for my doggerel!). It is important. Prose is the medium to communicate thoughts; poetry is the medium to convey feelings. So through the whole Bible (most prophecies are in poetic form).

God has feelings, too. His pleasure and pain are particularly clear in these first chapters. You may well feel the same as you read this account of our beginnings, particularly if you read it aloud, to yourself if not to someone else.

Genesis, Chapters 1 – 3

A long time ago, when nothing else existed, the God who had always been there brought the entire universe into being, the whole of outer space and this planet earth.

At first the earth was just a mass of fluid matter, quite uninhabitable and indeed uninhabited. It was shrouded in darkness and engulfed in water; but God's own spirit was hovering just above the flood.

Then God commanded: "Let the light in". And there it was! It looked just right to God, but he decided to alternate light with darkness, giving them different names: "day" and "night". The original darkness and the new light were the evening and the morning of God's first working day.

Then God spoke again: "Let there be two reservoirs of water, with an expanse between them". So he separated the water on the surface from the moisture in the atmosphere. That is how the 'sky', as God called it, came to be. This ended his second day's work.

The next thing God said was: "Let the surface water be concentrated in one area, so that the rest may dry out." Sure enough, it happened! From then on, God referred to "sea" and "land" separately. He liked what he saw and added: "Now let the land sprout vegetation, plants with seeds and trees with fruit, all able to reproduce themselves". And they appeared – all kinds of plant and tree, each able to propagate its own type. Everything fitted into God's plan. His third day's work was over.

Now God declared: "Let different sources of light appear in the sky. They will distinguish days from nights and make it possible to measure seasons, special days and years; though their main purpose will be to provide illumination." And so it is, just as he said. The two brightest lights are the larger "sun" that dominates the day and the lesser "moon" which predominates at night, surrounded by twinkling stars. God put them all there for earth's sake – to light it, regulate it and maintain the alternating pattern of light and darkness.

God was pleased that his fourth day's work had turned out so well.

The next order God issued was: "Let the sea and the sky teem with living creatures, with shoals of swimming fish and flocks of flying birds". So God brought into being all the animated things that inhabit the oceans, from huge monsters of the deep to the tiny organisms floating in the waves – and all the variety of birds and insects on the wing in the wind above. To God it was a wonderful sight and he encouraged them to breed and increase in numbers, so that every part of sea and sky might swarm with life. That ended his fifth day.

Then God announced: "Now let the land also teem with living creatures – mammals, reptiles and wildlife of every sort." As before, no sooner was it said than done! He made all kinds of wildlife, including mammals and reptiles, each as a distinct type. And they all gave him pleasure.

At this point God reached a momentous decision: "Now let's make some quite different creatures, more our kind – beings, just like us. They can be in charge of all the others – the fish in the sea, the birds of the air and the animals on the land."

To resemble himself God created mankind,
To reflect in themselves his own heart, will and mind,
To relate to each other, male and female entwined.

Then he affirmed their unique position with words

of encouragement: "Produce many offspring, for you are to occupy and control the whole earth. The fish in the sea, the birds of the air and the animals on the land are all yours to master. I am also giving you the seed-bearing plants and the fruit-bearing trees as your food supply. The birds and the beasts can have the green foliage for their food." And so it was.

God surveyed all his handiwork and he was very satisfied with it . . . everything so right, so beautiful . . . six days' work well done.

Outer space and planet earth were now complete. Since nothing more was needed, God took the next day off. That is why he designated every seventh day to be different from the others, set apart for himself alone – because on that day he was not busy with his daily work on creation.

This is how our universe was born and how everything in it came to be the way it is; when the God whose name is "Always" was making outer space and the planet earth, there was a time when there was no vegetation at all on the ground. And if there had been, there was neither any rain to irrigate it nor any man to cultivate it. But underground springs welled up to the surface and watered the soil. And the God "Always" had already laid out a stretch of parkland, east of here, a place called Eden, which means "Delight". He brought the first man there to live. The God "Always" had planted a great variety of trees in the park with beautiful foliage and delicious fruit. Right in the middle were two rather special trees; fruit from one of them could maintain life indefinitely while the fruit of the other gave the eater personal experience of doing right and wrong.

One river watered the whole area but divided into four branches as it left the park. One was called the Pishon and wound across the entire length of Havilah, the land where pure nuggets of gold were later found, as well as aromatic resin and onyx. The second was called the Gihon and meandered right through the country of Cush. The third was the present Tigris, which flows in front of the city of Asshur. The fourth was what we know as the Euphrates.

So the God "Always" set the man in this "Parkland of Delight" to develop and protect it. And the God "Always" gave him very clear orders: "You are perfectly free to eat the fruit of any tree except one – the tree that gives experience of right and wrong. If you taste that you will certainly have to die the death."

Then the God "Always" said to himself: "It isn't right for the man to be all on his own. I will provide a matching partner for him."

Now the God "Always" had fashioned all sorts of birds and beasts out of the soil and he brought them in contact with the man to see how he would describe them; and whatever the man said about each one became its name. So it was man who labelled all the other creatures but in none of them did he recognise a suitable companion for himself.

So the God "Always" sent the man into a deep coma and while he was unconscious God took some tissue from the side of his body, and pulled the flesh together over the gap. From the tissue he produced a female clone and introduced her to the man, who burst out with:

"At last you have granted my wish,
A companion of my bones and flesh,
"Woman" to me is her name,
Wooed by the man whence she came."

All this explains why a man lets go of his parents and holds on to his wife, their two bodies melting into one again.

The first man and his new wife wandered about the park quite bare, but without the slightest embarrassment.

Now there was a deadly reptile around, more cunning than any of the wild beasts the God "Always" had made. He chatted with the woman one day and asked, "You don't mean to tell me that God has actually forbidden you to eat any fruit from all these trees?" She replied, "No, it's not quite like that. We can eat fruit from the trees, but God did forbid us to eat from that one in the middle. In fact, he warned us that if we even touch it, we'll have to be put to death."

"Surely he wouldn't do that to you," said the reptile to the woman, "he's just trying to frighten you off because he knows perfectly well that when you eat that fruit you'd see things quite differently. Actually it would put you on the same level as him, able to decide for yourself what is right and wrong."

So she took a good look at the tree and noticed how nourishing and tasty the fruit appeared to be. Besides, it was obviously an advantage to be able to make one's own moral judgements. So she picked some, ate part and gave the rest to her husband, who was with her at the time and he promptly ate too. Sure enough, they did see things quite differently! For the first time they felt self-conscious about their nudity. So they tried to cover up with crude clothes stitched together from fig leaves.

That very evening they suddenly became aware of the approach of the God "Always" and ran to hide in the undergrowth. But the God "Always" called out to the man: "What have you got yourself into?" He answered: "I heard you coming and I was frightened because I haven't got any decent clothes. So I'm hiding in the bushes over here." Then God demanded, "How did you discover what it feels like to be naked? Have you been eating the fruit I ordered you to leave alone?" The man tried to defend himself: "It's all due to that woman you sent along; she brought this fruit to me, so naturally I just ate it without question."

Then the God "Always" challenged the woman: "What have you been up to?" The woman said, "It's that dreadful reptile's fault! He deliberately deluded me and I fell for it."

So the God "Always" said to the reptile: "As a punishment for your part in this –

Above all the beasts I will curse
Your ways with a fate that is worse!
On your belly you'll slither and thrust
With your mouth hanging down in the dust.
For the rest of the days of your life,
There'll be terror, hostility, strife
Between woman and you for this deed
Which you'll both pass along to your seed;
But his foot on your skull you will feel
As you strike out in fear at his heel."
Then to the woman he said:
"Let the pain of child-bearing increase
The agony, labour and stress;
You'll desire a man to control
But find yourself under his rule."

But to the man, Adam, he said, "Because you paid
attention to your wife rather than me and disobeyed my
order prohibiting that tree –

There's a curse on the soil;
All your days you will toil.
Thorns and thistles will grow
Among all that you sow.
With a brow running sweat
You will labour to eat;
Then return to the ground
In the state you were found.

20

From the clay you were made;
In the dust you'll be laid."

Adam gave his wife the name Eve (it means: "Life-giving") because he now realised she would be the mother of all human beings who would ever live.

The God "Always" made some new clothes from animal skins for Adam and his wife and got them properly dressed. Then the God "Always" said to himself, "Now that this man has become as conscious of good and evil things as we have been, how could we limit the damage if he is still able to eat from the other special tree and live as long as us?" To prevent this happening, the God "Always" banished him from the Park of Delight and sent him back to cultivate the very same patch of ground from which he was originally moulded!

After he had been expelled, heavenly angels were stationed on the eastern border of the Park of Delight, guarding access to the tree of continuous life with sharp, scorching weapons.

2

THE CROSS, THE CROOK, AND THE CROWN
(Psalms 22 – 24)

Introduction

To some, it will seem sacrilegious to meddle with the twenty-third psalm. The familiar words are certainly very beautiful – yet can hide the real meaning!

For example, the word "death" is not in the original Hebrew. This is a psalm for the whole of life, not the end of it. It is really quite inappropriate for funerals. John Bunyan was right to put the 'valley of deep darkness' in the middle of his *The Pilgrim's Progress*.

The shepherd has failed if the sheep die on him! It is his job to preserve life. The sheep rejoice in their provision, protection and prospect.

But I wanted to link this well-known psalm with the lesser known psalms on either side of it. They belong together.

Too many want the Lord to be their Shepherd in the present without seeing him as their Saviour in the past or their Sovereign in the future.

It is those who realise they are sinners and who become seekers who have the right to be singers.

It is Psalm 24 that ought to be read or sung at funerals.

It is a reminder that 'without holiness no-one will see the Lord' when he comes in glory. The shepherd has skilful hands and a caring heart; the sheep need clean hands and pure hearts.

This time I have used the phrase: 'who really exists' rather than "Always" for God's name, Yahweh.

Psalm 22

My God, my God, why?
Why have you left me all alone, me of all people?
Why do you seem so distant,
too far away to help me
or even to hear my groans?
O my God, I shout in the daylight,
but there's no reply from you;
I howl in the dark,
but no relief comes.
It doesn't make sense,
because you are utterly good,
lauded to the skies by this nation.
Our ancestors trusted you to the hilt;
and when they did,
you got them out of trouble.
They appealed to you –
and reached safety;
when they relied on you
they were never let down.

But I am treated more like a worm than a human
being,
with no consideration from men
and only contempt from the mob.
Everyone looking at me makes fun of me;
they put their tongues out,
shrug their shoulders and jeer:
"He said the Lord would prove him right;
see if he gets him out of this!
If the Lord's so fond of him,
let him set him free."
If they only knew –
you were the one who brought me safely through
childbirth
and you kept me safe while I was still being breast-
fed.
I have had to depend on you
since my life began;
And you have been my very own God
since my mother brought me into the world.
Don't leave me now when I'm in such peril,
for there is no-one else who can possibly help.
I'm in a bull-ring,
surrounded by the most ferocious beasts in the whole
country;
they bare their teeth, like a fierce, famished lion.
My strength is draining away,
my joints are being dislocated,
my heart beats like putty in my chest,

my body is as dry as baked clay,
my tongue is stuck to the roof of my mouth . . .
You're letting me disintegrate into dead dust.
A gang of crooks circle me like a pack of hounds;
they've already torn my hands and my feet.
My bones stand out clear enough to count,
but they just stare and gloat over me.
They've grabbed my clothes
and they're gambling for my shirt.
What do you think you're doing, Lord?
Don't remain aloof!
You're my only support!
Hurry back to my side!
Save my dear life from this violent end –
from the fangs of these dogs,
from the jaws of these lions,
from the horns of these bulls . . .
You've given me your answer!

I'll tell my brothers you've lived up to your name
again;
I'll be among them when they meet and share my
testimony.
Each one of you who fears this God Jehovah,
tell him how much you think of him.
Everyone who claims to be descended from Jacob,
give all the credit to him.
All who belong to the nation of Israel,
hold him in deep respect.

For he was neither too haughty nor too horrified
to get involved with the suffering of the underdog;
he didn't turn his back on him,
but listened to his cry for help.
You will give praise to me
in the large congregation;
and I will keep the promises I made to you,
as reverent eyes will see.
Those who suffered will be satisfied;
those who have been seekers will become singers.
May this thrilling experience last for ever.
In every corner of the world,
people will think about God again
and come back to him.
Different races and nations
will be really united
in worshipping him.
For the Lord controls the world
and is in charge of all international affairs.
Yes, even the top people will bow to his superiority,
for they are but mortals heading for the grave
and nobody can hold on to his life indefinitely.
Future generations will take over his work,
for men will talk about this God who really exists
to their children who come after them.
His liberation will be announced
to those whose lives haven't even started yet;
they will be told that God has worked it all out
and it is finished!

Psalm 23

The only God who really exists,
the God of the Jews,
cares for me as an individual,
like a shepherd for his sheep;
so that I'll never lack anything
that I really need.
He forces me to rest,
where there is abundant nourishment;
then he moves me on,
making sure I have constant refreshment.
He puts new life into me
when I'm exhausted.
He keeps me on the right track,
to maintain his good reputation.
Even if I travel through a deep dark ravine,
where danger lurks in the shadows,
I'm not afraid of coming to any harm,
because you are right there beside me.
With your cudgel to guard and your crook to guide,
I feel quite safe.
You lay the table for me,
in full view of my helpless foes;
you treat me as an honoured guest
and put on a lavish spread.
For the rest of my days nothing will chase after me –

except your generous and undeserved kindness
and I'll be at home with this God,
as long as I live.

Psalm 24

The God of the Jews owns this planet,
with everything in it
and everyone on it;
because he built up the land from the bed of the
ocean
and sent down the water that flows in its rivers.
But who could scale his holy height?
And who could stay in his perfect presence?
Only one whose conduct was faultless
and whose character was flawless;
who had not based his life on things that don't ring
true
and who had never broken his word.
Such a man would be given attention and approval
by the God who saved him.
For people like this really want to find God
and meet him face to face, as Jacob did.

(Pause for a moment and think about yourself)

Fling wide the city gates!
Open up the old citadel doors!

His magnificent Majesty is about to enter!
Who is this marvellous monarch?
The powerful God of the Jews,
the undefeated God of Israel!
Fling wide the city gates!
Open up those old citadel doors!
His magnificent Majesty is about to enter!
Who is this marvellous monarch?
The God who commands all the forces of the
universe –
that's who this marvellous monarch is!

(Be quiet for a while and think about him).

3

TIME AND TIDE
(Ecclesiastes 3:1–8)

Introduction

I was preaching a series of sermons on this neglected, even despised, book. To my delight, it proved to have an unexpected appeal and influence. A number of hearers came to faith in Christ, including some of his own Jewish people.

At the same time there was a television documentary series about the Royal Navy's last aircraft carrier, which captured the nation's interest. Its theme music was the song: "When I'm sailing", by Rod Stewart. The melody was so catchy, many of us got it "on the brain" and I found myself humming it when I worked in my study. While reading the best-known and most-quoted passage of Solomon's autobiographical testimony, words and music came together quite spontaneously. This song was the result.

Ecclesiastes 3:1–8

God is sovereign,
Sets the seasons:
Date of birthday,
Day of death.
Time for planting,
Time for reaping;
Time for killing,
Time to heal.
Time for wrecking,
Time for building;
Time for sorrow,
Time for job.
Time for mourning,
Time for dancing;
Time for kissing,
Time to stop!

Time for finding,
Time for losing;
Time for saving,
Time for waste.
Time for tearing,
Time for mending;
Time for silence,
Time to talk.

Time for loving,
Time for hating;
Time for fighting,
Time for peace.
Have your fun, then,
But remember . . .
God is sovereign;
HE decrees.

4

ODE TO JOY
(Habakkuk 3)

Introduction

The three chapters of this 'minor' prophet may be seen as examples of prophetic prayer, preaching and praise.

When Habakkuk complained that God was doing nothing about Jerusalem's spiritual and moral decline, he was shocked to be told that an impending Babylonian invasion was the divine solution! He then criticised this action as too severe because the whole population would be indiscriminately annihilated, but was assured that "the righteous will survive by keeping faith" with their God. Commissioned to warn his people of impending doom by large-print hoardings, the prophet came to the point where he could sing the praise of God even in the coming disaster.

The Babylonians were notorious for their 'scorched earth' policy, destroying animals and even trees, as well as people (note the reference to the absence of sheep, cattle, figs, grapes and olives).

The chapter begins with a musical direction, so I put it into modern verse, but could not find any tune of the right metre. On a visit to South Africa I learned that it would fit their national anthem, but for obvious reasons

I was not allowed to use it. On moving to Zimbabwe, I learned that the former Rhodesian national anthem was right for the words – Beethoven's "Ode to Joy" from his 9th Symphony (with the repetition of the third and fourth lines).

So I came back to England with words and music. Imagine my surprise on learning that a fellowship in the north of England had been told (in a word of prophecy) to learn this very tune but to wait until the words were given to them. They were getting rather tired of the melody without lyrics and even made one futile attempt to write them. Imagine their excitement when their pastor brought my verses back from a conference where I recited them.

Habakkuk, Chapter 3

(1)

Lord your fame has gone before you
From the time your arm was bared;
Tales of deeds so overwhelming
Even listening makes me scared:
Now, today, O Lord, repeat them
Prove that you are still the same –
But in wrath remember mercy
For the honour of your name.
Look! This holy God descending

Spreads the sky with glorious rays,
Trailing from his hand of power –
Earth is filled with sounds of praise.

(2)

But the guilty nations tremble,
Plague and pestilence their fears;
Even ancient mountains crumble
When the infinite appears.
Are you angry with the rivers?
Is your wrath upon the streams?
Do you rage against the oceans
With your horse and chariot teams?
Writhing hills and flooded valleys,
Sun and moon stand still with fear
At the glint of flying arrows,
Lightning of your flashing spear.

(3)

Striding through the earth in vengeance,
Threshing nations till it's done –
You have come to save your people,
Rescue your anointed one:
As you crush their wicked leader
And their gloating troops depart –
Great emotion grips my body,
Quivering lips and pounding heart,
Trembling legs give way beneath me –
Yet with patience will I wait

When the foe invades my country,
Certain of his dreadful fate.

(4)

Though the fig tree does not blossom
And the vine is void of grapes,
Though the olive trees are barren
And the fields produce no crops,
Though no lambs are in the sheepfold
And no cattle in the stall –
Yet will I enjoy my Saviour,
Glad that God is all in all.
Like a deer whose feet are leaping,
On the heights my spirit soared;
Life is mine by keeping faithful
To this righteous Sovereign Lord!

5

TWO MEN AND THEIR MONEY
(Luke 15–16)

Introduction

Who has not heard about "the prodigal son"? Yet the very familiarity with this memorable parable can blind us to its real content and context, which my paraphrase seeks to draw out.

It is really about a prodigal father, who gives his money to an irresponsible son and an insensitive son, long before they could normally expect it. It is the story of two lost sons – one like the sheep lost far away and aware of it, the other like the coin lost at home and unaware of it. The father goes out to meet both, but only succeeds in winning the love of one.

The real-life situation in which Jesus told the story, reveals that the main emphasis is not on the younger brother (the publicans and sinners) but the elder (the Pharisees and scribes). They were refusing to join the celebratory feast to welcome those Jesus (who is represented by the 'father' in the tale and who represents the father in reality) has "found".

There is also a remarkable parallel between the two brothers in chapter 15 and the two men in chapter 16.

Money is the connecting link and both the younger brother and the crooked agent "waste" it (the word is the same). Both came to their senses and acted accordingly, ensuring their secure future; both learned that relationships matter more than possessions.

The older brother and the rich man have a lot in common too. Neither was guilty of sin, vice or crime – just indulgence, indifference and independence. They both end up alone.

Luke, Chapters 15 and 16

Some time later the spiritual outcasts, some simply irreligious and others downright immoral, gathered around Jesus to hear what he had to say. But the Pharisees and the legal scholars criticised him for associating with them and muttered among themselves: "This fellow seems to enjoy the company of those who don't even try to keep God's laws – he actually has meals with them!" So Jesus defended his action by telling them a story:

Which of you men, he began, owning a flock of one hundred sheep and losing one of them, wouldn't leave the ninety-nine in the open field where they were and search everywhere for the lost one until he has found it again? And when he does find it, he's so happy he thinks nothing of carrying it all the way back on his shoulders. When he gets it home, he invites all his friends and neighbours: "Come and celebrate with me – I've found that sheep I'd lost!" I'm telling you: it's exactly the same in heaven; there's more excitement up there over a single sinner who's brought back from his wilful wandering than over ninety-nine respectable citizens who never put a foot wrong!

Or what woman owning a valuable pendant with ten silver tokens and losing one of them, wouldn't get a torch and brush and search every nook and cranny until she has found it again? And when she does find it, she's so happy she invites all her friends and neighbours: "Come and celebrate with me. I just found that coin I'd lost!" I'm telling you it's exactly the same among God's angels; they also celebrate every time just one sinner has a change of heart.

Then Jesus added: There was once a man with two sons. The younger one went to his father and demanded: "Dad, I want my share of the business now, before you die." So the father divided his assets between the two brothers. Not long afterwards the younger son turned his capital into cash and went abroad. There he squandered his fortune on an extravagant life-style. Just when he had spent all his money, that country was hit by a bad harvest which led to severe shortage of food. Prices rocketed and he soon felt the pinch. To stay alive, he hung around a local landowner who let him cart swill to the pigs. Often he longed to stuff his own stomach from the same trough, but no-one even thought of giving him anything. When he finally came to his senses, he said to himself: "Just think – all those hired hands on my father's farm have more than enough to eat while here I am, starving to death. I'd better get back to my father again. I'll just say to him: "I realise I've done a terrible wrong, both against God and against you. I'm not fit to be regarded as your son again but how about taking me onto the payroll with the other employees?" So he set off home. But while he still had some way to go, his father spotted him coming. He was moved to his depths and ran out to meet him, threw his arms around his neck and kept kissing him. The son began his prepared speech: "Dad, I realise I've been terribly wrong, from God's viewpoint as well as yours – I just don't deserve to be regarded as your son any more . . ." But his father interrupted him, turned to the servants who had come to see what was happening and ordered them: "Bring my best suit and get him properly dressed, put my signet ring on his finger and get some shoes for his feet. And slaughter that calf we've been fattening up. We must have a big meal to celebrate such an occasion. My son was as good as dead to me and he's come back into my life again. I thought I'd lost him but we've found each other again!" So the festivities got under way.

All this time the elder son had been out working in the fields. As he approached the family home at the end of the day, he heard sounds of a party – singing and dancing to a band. So he summoned one of the lads standing around and asked what it was all in aid of. He blurted out: "Your brother's back and your father has slaughtered the calf you were fattening because he's home safe and sound." The elder brother was furious and refused to go anywhere near. So out rushed the father for the second time that day, to appeal to him to change his attitude. But he exploded with anger: "Look at all the years I've been slaving for you here! Never once have I disobeyed your orders or gone against your wishes. Yet you never even let me kill a baby goat to have a good time with my pals. But as soon as this son of yours turns up, having swallowed up your hard-earned savings in brothels, then you go and kill the best animal on the farm in his honour!" But the father gently replied: "My dear boy, you were the one who stayed here by my side and you know that the remaining estate is already made over to you. Don't you understand that we just had to have a celebration. For here was your brother, who's been as good as dead to us and now he's living with us again. I thought we'd lost him for ever but now we've found each other again . . . ."

Jesus went on to tell another story to his own followers: Once upon a time there was a wealthy man who employed an agent to manage his estate; and reports reached him that this man was embezzling his capital. So he sent for the man and faced him with it. "What's all this I keep hearing about you. I'm going to have your accounts audited right away. I can't keep you on as manager." So the agent considered his future prospects. "What can I possibly do for a living," he said to himself, "now that the boss has given me the sack? I'll make sure that when I am out of a job there'll be plenty of my former clients who'll want to help me out." So he sent for every tenant who had an outstanding debt to his employer. To the first one who came, he said, "How much do you owe my boss?" "Four thousand litres of oil," he replied. Then the agent said, "Here is the original contract. Quick, sit down here and alter the figure to two thousand." Later, he said to another, "You there, how much did you agree to pay?" He replied, "Two hundred sacks of wheat." So the agent said, "Here's your agreement; you can cut the figure down by a fifth." When the landlord heard about these revised contracts, he couldn't help congratulating the dishonest agent for his quick thinking and shrewd move.

Sadly it is often the case that those who only live for what this world offers show more sense in their business dealings with other people than those who have been enlightened about the other world. So, said Jesus, my advice to you is this: use the world's dirty money to make sure you have plenty, so that when you finally leave all your assets behind, they will welcome you with open arms into heaven itself.

The man who is trustworthy in trifling matters will have the same integrity in big deals too. And the man who cheats over small amounts will be just as crooked in big business. So if you can't be trusted to handle a corruptible commodity like money, who is going to let you look after anything of really lasting value? And if you are unreliable in looking after other people's assets, who will ever think of giving you some of your own?

No employee can ever work wholeheartedly for two employers. He is bound to make comparisons and will like one better than the other or be more loyal to one, while being less concerned for the other. That's why you cannot devote yourself to making money and serving God at the same time.

Some Pharisees overheard these remarks of Jesus to his disciples. They managed to be both rich and religious and they sneered at his statement. But he knew what they were thinking and told them: you may convince your colleagues, but God sees right through you! Men may be impressed but God is disgusted.

The commandments of Moses and the accusations of the prophets were in force right up to the arrival of John the Baptiser; since then the rule of God has been inaugurated and people are seizing the opportunity to live under it. In fact, it would be easier for planet earth and outer space to disappear than for one iota of divine legislation to be annulled.

To give you just one example: in God's sight, whoever divorces his wife and marries someone else is living in adultery; and whoever marries a divorced woman also commits adultery.

There was once a wealthy man, who used to wear the most expensive suits and enjoy lavish meals every day of his life. And there was a poor beggar who sat in the gutter just outside his drive gates, appropriately named:

God-help-us. His wretched body was a mass of ulcers and he would have given anything just to eat what was thrown into the waste bin up at the house. Stray dogs in the neighbourhood used to lick the matter oozing from his sores. In the course of time, the beggar died and his spirit was escorted by the angels into the loving embrace of Abraham. Shortly after that, the wealthy man passed away and a very impressive funeral took place. But he himself did not attend it. He was already suffering in hell.

In his agony, he glanced up and spotted Abraham in the far distance, and he was hugging that old beggar, God-help-us! "Father Abraham," he shouted, "Have pity on me. I'd even suck that beggar's finger if he'd dip it in some water first! This heat is unbearable." But Abraham solemnly replied, "Just recall how comfortable your life was and how miserable was the lot of my friend, God-help-us. Now it is time for him to have a bit of comfort and for you to know what it is to suffer. In any case, there's a huge canyon between us. No-one can cross from here to there and no-one can get from there to here."

So the poor rich man thought of another possibility. "I plead with you then, Father Abraham. If you can't send anyone over here, please send someone to my home on earth. At least my five brothers could be warned about this dreadful place." But Abraham shook his head and pointed out: "They have a Bible in the house. If they just read what Moses and the prophets had to say, they'll have all the warning they need." But the condemned man disagreed. "That's not enough to convince them, Father Abraham. But if someone came back from the grave to tell them what really happens, they'd surely change their ways." But Abraham simply said, "If they won't pay any attention to the words God gave through Moses and the other prophets, they are hardly likely to believe someone who tells them he's returned from among the dead."

6

THE REASON WHY
(John 1)

Introduction

Mark began the story of Jesus with his baptism at thirty. Matthew went back to his birth, his conception and beyond, to Abraham. Luke went back further still, to Adam. But John began at "the beginning" of our universe, the furthest our minds can go back. And the eternal, pre-existent Son of God was already there, as he always had been.

But what to call him? "Jesus" was a human name, given when he became a human being. What name can we use for him before that? John, writing in his old age and in Ephesus, boldly borrowed a word from the history of that very city.

Centuries before, a man called Heraclitus had laid the foundations of science by encouraging his pupils to use observation and deduction in order to discover "the reason why" things are as they are. This "reason why", or LOGOS, to use his Greek word, is the basis for our knowledge in every sphere – hence: biology, zoology, psychology, sociology, geology, meteorology, etc. But for him the 'logos' was a thing, a force, a law.

Later, Philo, a Jewish teacher in the university of Alexandria, 'personified' the Logos (much as the book of Proverbs calls Wisdom 'she').

John defined the Logos behind the whole universe as possessing eternity, personality, deity and humanity – and to be identified with Jesus of Nazareth. He is the 'reason' our universe exists and ourselves in it!

This passage ranks with a few others in the New Testament (notably Colossians 1:15-20 and Hebrews 1:1-4) as a statement about the Lord Jesus Christ which makes him absolutely unique. It is impossible to put him in the pantheon of comparative religion alongside other figures like Confucius, Buddha or Mohammed.

John, Chapter 1

At the very first moment of its existence, the whole reason for our universe was already there and had been there from all eternity. Both the purpose and pattern of it all were to be found in a person, someone who could look God in the face because he, too, was fully divine. From the start of what we call "Time", he was working alongside the Creator. It was through this partnership that everything else came into being; in fact, not one thing was made without his personal involvement. Even life itself originated in him and his own life sheds light on the meaning of life for every member of the human race. His light goes on shining through all the gloom of human history, because no amount of darkness can ever extinguish it.

In the course of time a man appeared with special commission from God himself. His name was John and he came to announce the imminent appearance of this light of life, so that everyone could put their faith in God by getting to know this person. John himself could not enlighten anyone but God sent him to point out the one who would. The real illumination was already entering the world at that very time and was going to show everybody up by shining among them. He came right into this world, the world he himself had brought into being – yet the world didn't recognise him for who he was! He arrived at his very own place, but his own people wouldn't give him a welcome. However, some did accept him, using his name with utter confidence, and these were given his authority to regard themselves as God's new family – which, indeed, they now were by birth, not because of their physical beginnings, whether that was a result of impulsive urge or deliberate choice, but by the direct act of God.

So this divine person, who was the reason behind our whole universe, changed into a human being and pitched his tent among ours. We were spectators of his dazzling brilliance, which could only have radiated from God's very own Son, shot through with generosity and integrity.

John was a reliable witness and shouted to the crowds: "This is the person I've been telling you about.

I told you that my successor would take precedence over me, because he was around before I was even born".

And we also have benefited so much from all that he had in such full measure, receiving one undeserved favour after another. All we got through Moses were strict rules which we had to try to keep; but the help and the honesty we needed to live right came through Jesus, the real Messiah. Nobody had ever before had the chance to see God as he really is; now God's very own Son, who has been closer to his Father than anyone else, has shown us everything we need to know about him.

7

LICENCE, LIBERTY AND LEGALISM
(Galatians)

Introduction

This letter has been called 'The Magna Carta of Christian Liberty'. What is not always realised is that Paul is fighting on two fronts, the opposite dangers of licence and legalism. Both lead to a loss of true freedom and a return to slavery, either in bondage to one's own wrong desires or the rules of others.

I felt I needed to re-translate it for two reasons. One was intellectual. Paul's arguments are quite profound, even obscure. I wanted to be sure I understood his case. The other was emotional. This is Paul's hottest letter! Few translations conveyed the temperature. He was highly indignant that his hard work was so quickly being undone by others. But his anger was not self-centred; he was primarily concerned for his converts.

If they were governed by either the flesh or the law, they would lose the liberty of the Spirit. They would produce works, but not fruit.

Circumcision figures prominently because submission to this would put them under obligation to keep all six hundred and thirteen laws of Moses! It is significant that he never once argues that baptism has taken the place of the Jewish rite; one is of faith, the other is of flesh.

Polite English versions for reading in church usually avoid some of Paul's cruder expressions (for example, 'dung' in Philippians 3:8 is an earthy word for human excreta, for which there is an exact Anglo-Saxon equivalent!). I have restored these, for they have a salutary effect in stabbing us awake, making it hard to 'kick against the pricks' of conscience.

Martin Luther and John Bunyan, both of whom were masters of blunt language, had a high regard for this letter. They realised how vital its message was for true Christian living. Had Paul not written it, or fought for our freedom, Christianity might have simply become another religion among many, instead of the greatest liberating force the world has seen.

For true freedom may be simply defined. It is the freedom not to sin, the freedom to live right. And it can only be found in Christ, through his Spirit.

Galatians

From Paul, the Lord's emissary (not appointed by any group of human officials or even by divine guidance through a human agent, but personally sent by Jesus the Messiah and God his father, who brought him back to life after his burial). All the Christian brothers here have read and approved my letter.

To: the gatherings of God's people in the province of Galatia.

May you all enjoy the undeserved generosity and total harmony of God our Father and his Son Jesus, our Lord and Messiah. Our bad deeds cost him his life, but he gave it willingly to rescue us from the immorality of our contemporary scene. The plan of escape was decided by our Father-God, who should never cease to get the credit. So be it.

I am shattered to discover that already all of you are deserting this God who picked you out for his special offer of Christ's free gift and swinging to a different gospel, which is not even "good news". You are being muddled by certain people who aim to turn the gospel upside down. But listen – if we ourselves, or even a supernatural messenger from the other world, should bring a message to you that contradicts what I have already delivered, may he be damned! We told you this before, but I must repeat it – if anyone at all preaches a gospel that varies from the one you first accepted, then to hell with him!

Now does that sound like someone who is trying to get on the right side of men, or of God? Am I being accused of seeking popularity? If I still wanted to please people, the last thing I would be is one of Christ's workers.

My dear brothers, I must make it quite clear to all of you that the Good News I tell is no human tale. I neither heard others relating it, nor did anyone pass it on to me. I got it direct from Jesus the Messiah, as the events of my life prove.

You must have heard about my earlier career in the Jewish religion. In my extreme fanaticism I was hunting down God's company of Christian believers and playing havoc with them. As an ardent supporter of Judaism, I forged ahead of many fellow-nationals of my own age, because I was so enthusiastic about the established customs of my ancestors.

Then God took a hand. He had marked me out before I left my mother's womb and generously chose me of all people to show others what his Son was really like, especially those I used to call foreigners. At once I decided not to seek anybody's advice. So I did not go to Jerusalem to consult those who were already working as emissaries of the Lord. Instead I went off alone into the Arabian desert to think it all over; and from there I returned straight to Damascus.

It was not until three years later that I finally got to know Peter in Jerusalem. Even then I only stayed two weeks and saw none of the other apostles, though I did meet James, our divine leader's own brother (as God watches what I write, I'm not making any of this up). After that I went to various places in Syria and Cilicia, so the Christian gatherings in Judea would still not have recognised my face. All they knew of me was hearsay – that their bitter enemy was now spreading the very beliefs he had tried so hard to wreck – and they thanked God for the transformation.

Another fourteen years passed before I paid another visit to Jerusalem. This time Barnabas and Titus went with me. It was God who prompted me to go and have a private discussion with the reputed leaders of the Jewish Christians. I intended to check with them the gospel I had been spreading among other nations, lest all my efforts were being wasted. I took Titus as a kind of test case, for he was a Greek Christian. But they never once insisted that he go through the initiation rite of being circumcised. In fact, the question would never have arisen but for some interlopers who had no right to be in the meeting at all. They sneaked in to spy on the freedom we enjoy in our relationship with Christ; they were looking for some way of getting us back under the control of their system. But not for one minute did we give way to their demands, or you would have lost what is truly good news. As far as the apparent leaders were concerned (their exact position doesn't bother me, for God pays no attention to status; I mean those who were obviously looked up to by the others), they added nothing whatever to the teaching I had outlined. On the contrary, they could see that I was as qualified to take the good news to uncircumcised people as Peter had been to the circumcised. For the same God who was working so effectively through Peter's outreach to the Jews was obviously doing the same through mine to the Gentiles. James, John and Cephas (Peter was using his Hebrew name) seemed to be the three mainstays and when they realised how much God was blessing my work, they shook hands with Barnabas and myself as a token of full partnership, on the understanding that they would concentrate on the Jews and we on the non-Jews. The only plea they made was that we should not forget to send financial aid to poor Jewish Christians and I was more than ready to go on with this.

But a serious crisis arose when Peter returned our visit and came to Antioch. I had to oppose him to his face, for he was clearly in the wrong. When he first came, he was quite happy to eat with the Gentile converts. Then some colleagues of James arrived and Peter was afraid of what they might think, so he began to have his meals separately. The other Jewish believers pretended to agree with him and even my friend Barnabas was swept into the hypocrisy. When I saw that such behaviour could not be squared with the reality of the gospel, I said to Peter in front of everybody, "You are a Jewish national, but you dropped your scruples and adopted the lifestyle of Gentile foreigners. Why all of a sudden are you now trying to make them accept Jewish customs?"

We were born within God's chosen people and not among the lawless outsiders of other nations. Yet we know perfectly well that a man cannot be innocent in God's sight by trying to obey the commandments but only by trusting Jesus Christ to take away his sins. So even we Jews had to get right with God by relying on the work of Jesus the Messiah rather than on our own attempts to live up to God's standards. Our sacred writings freely admit that 'judged by God's laws, no man living could ever be acquitted' (Psalm 143:2). But suppose our quest to be right with God through Christ does find us living outside the Jewish law. Does that make Christ an anarchist, deliberately encouraging lawlessness? Never!

What would really make me a lawbreaker would be to erect again the whole legal system I demolished. I discovered long ago that trying to keep God's laws was a deadly business. The failure killed my ego – but that gave me the very break I needed to live as God wanted me to. For when I realised that Jesus died on the cross for me, the person I used to be died as well. I know I'm still around, but it's not really me; "it's Christ living his life in me. So the real life I'm now living in this mortal body springs from continual trust in God's son, who loved me so much he sacrificed his life for me. Whatever anyone else does, I'm not going to be the one to make God's generosity redundant. For if I could get to heaven by keeping the commandments, then Christ's death is utterly meaningless".

You stupid Galatians! Who has hoodwinked you, so that you no longer act on what is true? Your eyes were fastened on Jesus Christ by our vivid description of his death by crucifixion. Just answer me one simple question – when you first experienced God's Spirit, was that because you had done what the law demands or because you believed what you heard?

Right! Then have you gone out of your mind? Having

got started by the supernatural power of God's Spirit, do you think you can reach the finish by the natural energy of your own constitution?

Have you learned nothing from all you've been through? Surely you won't throw it all away now. Tell me, when God went on giving you a liberal supply of his Spirit, so that real miracles were happening among you, was this while you were trying to obey his laws or while you listened to what he said with complete trust?

Your experience is identical with Abraham's, for he "believed that God could do what he promised, and because of this trust he was listed in God's records as a good man" (Genesis 15:6). You realise, then that the true descendants of Abraham are those who have this same trust in God. And the Bible, looking forward to the days when God would accept other races on exactly the same basis of faith, includes the announcement of this good news to Abraham himself – "Through you all the peoples of the world will enjoy God's blessing with this man Abraham, who was so full of faith".

But those who rely on keeping the commandments are actually under God's curse, not his blessing. For the law of Moses states quite clearly that "anyone who fails to keep all the rules of this book all the time will be cursed" (Deuteronomy 27:26). It is patently obvious that nobody could possibly reach such a standard, if this is how God looks at us. So even the Old Testament points to another way to get right with God – "The good man will live by trusting" (Habakkuk 2:4). The law never mentions this matter of believing, its emphasis is all on achieving – "The man who obeys these rules will live well" (Leviticus 18:5).

Christ has ransomed us from this binding curse of the law and the price was to be cursed in our place. Quite literally, he paid the supreme penalty of the law – "The body of a man under God's curse is to be hanged on the bough of a tree" (Deuteronomy 21:23). By removing the curse in this way, Jesus our Messiah released the blessing of Abraham to non-Jews. So we could now receive the promised power of the Spirit, simply by believing.

Brothers, all this is nothing out of the ordinary: I can illustrate what has happened from everyday human affairs. Once a man's will has been sealed, it cannot be cancelled nor can any other provisions be added. Now God made his testament in favour of Abraham "and his issue" (Genesis 22:18). Just note that the word is singular rather than plural, indicating one surviving descendant rather than many; actually it referred to Christ. But my main point is this – an agreement already ratified by God cannot be cancelled by a legal code introduced four hundred and thirty years later, or else the promise was worthless. The two are incompatible. If the blessing is now inherited by keeping the commandments, it is no longer available on the original terms. But God generously gave that first promise to Abraham and he will always stand by it.

Then what was the point of the law? It was a

temporary addition to deal with human lawlessness! Until Abraham's "issue" arrived to inherit the promised blessing, wrongdoing had to be exposed for what it was and kept under some control.

Unlike the promise, the law was not given direct to men. God communicated it through heavenly messengers and an earthly intermediary handed it on. Normally a middleman is used to negotiate between two parties; and in a sense the law was a mutual contract, in that the conditions had to be accepted by the people. But our belief is that God stands alone. He is not an equal to be bargained with, but can act entirely on his own terms, as he did in giving the promise direct.

Do these differences mean that God introduced two rival religious systems, the law as an alternative to the promise? Never! If passing a law could make people live good lives, then legislation would be the answer. But the laws of the Bible simply shut down this possibility by proving that everybody does wrong, leaving the only way out that of believing God's promise by trusting in Jesus the Messiah.

Until the opportunity of faith came, we had to be remanded in custody and kept under the strong guard of the law, waiting for the day when we would be shown how to believe. Putting it another way, we were like children and the law was a strict guardian, keeping us under firm discipline until Christ could take over and put us right through our trust in him. Believing in Jesus Christ brought the full status and freedom which belongs to grown-up sons of God.

All of you who were initiated into the Christian life by immersion in water are now wrapped up in Christ. So you are no longer separate individuals – one a Jew and another a Greek, one a slave and another free, one male and another female. All of you make up just one person inside Jesus. As parts of Christ you belong to him, which makes you that single descendant of Abraham who is entitled to claim the blessing promised to his "issue".

Look at it like this – a child can inherit a business, but as long as he is under age he is no better off than one of the employees, even though he owns the whole lot. He is supervised by guardians and his affairs are managed by trustees, until the date set by his father. In much the same way, when we were spiritual infants, our behaviour was governed by the world's childish superstitions.

But God had appointed a time for our coming-of-age and when it was ripe, He sent his Son into our world. He came in the same way as we did, from a woman's body. She was a Jew, so he was born subject to the law. This enabled him to purchase the freedom of those who lived under its tyranny and give us the full status of grown-up sons.

Because you too have been recognised as God's sons, he sent the Spirit of his Son into our inmost beings, so that we call out instinctively, "Abba! Dad!" (which is exactly how Jesus addressed his heavenly Father). This proves that each of you is a son of God and no longer his servant; and if you are his son you are also his heir, and he will make sure you get the estate.

There was a time when you had no personal relationship with God. But your religion bound you to do so much for "gods" who weren't even real! But now that you know God as he is (or rather, now that he has introduced himself to you) how can you possibly go back to those feeble and needy superstitions? Do you really want to be in their grip again? Already you're observing a calendar of so-called "sacred" days and months and seasons and years. I am beginning to have a horrible fear that all my efforts to help you have been wasted.

My brothers, I beg you, please stand with me. After all, I was willing to identify with you. You've never hurt me before. You know it was because of physical illness that I first came to tell you the good news. My condition must have been a real trial to you, but you never made fun of it nor were you disgusted with me. Indeed, you gave me a welcome fit for a heavenly messenger or even the Messiah Jesus himself. You were so pleased and proud to have me. Where have all those feelings gone? I recall vividly that you wished it was possible to donate your eyes for transplanting in me. Now you seem to suspect me of being your enemy. Is that because I have been so honest with you?

I know these others are so keen to make a fuss of you; but their motives are not good. They want to have you all to themselves, so that you will make a fuss of them.

Don't get me wrong – special attention is always fine, provided the intentions are right. You are my special concern, even when I am not actually with you. My own children, I feel like a mother struggling with the pains of childbirth until Christ is brought right out in your lives. I just wish I could be with you at this moment so that you could hear the change in my tone of voice. I really am at my wit's end to know what to do about you.

Tell me this – you seem to have such a strong urge to be governed by the law of Moses, but have you really listened to everything it says? Take this one recorded incident:

Abraham was the father of two sons by two women, one a slave-girl and the other free. The slave-girl's boy was the natural result of a physical act; but the child of the free woman only came as the supernatural result of a divine promise. This contrast is intended to picture spiritual realities, for the two sons represent two very different kinds of relationship with God.

One stems from Mount Sinai and its children are born into bondage. Their symbolic mother is the slave-girl Hagar, whose connections were with Arabia, where Mount Sinai stands. She corresponds to the present Jewish capital of Jerusalem, whose leaders and subjects are under oppression. But there is another "Jerusalem" of heavenly origin, represented by the free woman, and she is the mother of all of us who believe. The Bible says of her, "Celebrate, you barren woman who never had a child; burst into cries of joy, you who never knew the pain of labour; for the lonely wife will have a far bigger family than she who has her husband" (Isaiah 54:1).

My brothers, we are like Isaac, for our life was brought into being by a divine promise. As in his day, the child born in the normal course of nature bullied the one born by the power of God's Spirit, so it is today. But look what the Bible says about the outcome of this: "Throw out the slave-girl and her son, for he will never share the father's property with the son of the free woman" (Genesis 21:10). So, brothers, get this quite clear in your minds – we are not the children of a slave-girl but of a free woman.

When Christ set us free, that was real freedom! So hang on to it and don't get tied up again in the chains of slavery. Listen! I, Paul, a Jewish Christian, make this serious statement – if you get circumcised, Christ himself will be of no more value to you. Let me repeat that. I give my solemn assurance to anyone who submits to the initiation ceremony of circumcision, that he has put himself under an obligation to obey every single statute of the Jewish law. The operation will not only cut off part of your body; it will cut you off from Christ! Any of you who tries to get right with God by keeping the commandments will find you have slipped beyond the range of God's undeserved mercy.

We Christians build our hopes on a very different basis. By the help of God's Spirit we wait expectantly for that right standing and state which result from trusting in Jesus the Messiah. Once we are part of him, it doesn't count for anything whether we are circumcised or uncircumcised. The only thing that matters is the kind of believing that is expressed in loving.

You were racing ahead in the Christian life. Who caused an obstruction and stopped you from putting the truth into practice? That kind of plausible persuasion never comes from God, who always calls you to press on. As they say, "It doesn't take much yeast to taint a large lump of dough". Yet somehow the Lord gives me the confidence that you are not going to change your outlook. As for the person who is disturbing you, he will one day have to take his punishment, whatever his position is now.

Regarding myself, brothers, I gather I am supposed to be preaching the need to be circumcised, even after all this time. If that were really true, how can anyone explain the violent opposition I encounter at the hands of other Jews? If I was advocating their laws, they wouldn't be so offended when I speak about the cross. I just wish that those who are agitating to cut off your foreskins would go the whole hog and castrate themselves!

So, my brothers, God meant you to be free. On the other hand, don't make this freedom an excuse for indulging your old self. Use it to show your love for others by putting yourselves at their service. For the whole law can be expressed in just one principle, namely, "You are to care for your fellow-man as much

as you do about yourself" (Leviticus 19:18). But if you
snap at each other and pull each other to pieces, watch
out that you don't end up by exterminating each other
altogether!

The approach I'm advocating is to let God's Spirit
decide each step you take. Then you just won't try to
satisfy the desires of your old self, whose cravings are
diametrically opposed to what God's Spirit wants – and
vice-versa. The two are incompatible, which is why
you find you can't always do what you really want to.
If the Spirit is leading your life, you have nothing to
fear from the law.

When the old self is at work, the results are pretty
obvious. It may produce promiscuity, dirty mindedness
or indecency. It is behind occultism and drug addiction.
It shows up in hatred, quarrelling, jealousy, temper,
rivalry, prejudice, and envy. It leads to binges, orgies
and things like that. I've warned you before, people
who go on doing this sort of thing will have no share
in God's coming reign.

When God's Spirit is at work, a fruit appears in
the character. Each cluster includes loving care, deep
happiness and quiet serenity; endless patience, practical
kindness and unstinted generosity; steady reliability,
gentle humility and firm self-control. No law has ever
been passed forbidding such virtues! They have room
to grow because those who belong to Christ have nailed
their old self to the cross, together with all its passions
and appetites.

If God's Spirit is leading our lives, let the same Spirit keep us in step with each other. We get out of step when our hollow pride wants a reputation of being ahead, regards others as rivals and is envious of their progress.

Brothers, if anyone slips up and is caught doing wrong, those of you who are spiritually mature should get him on his feet again. But handle him gently and humbly, keeping an eye on yourself, for sudden temptation could just as easily hit you.

When the strain is too much, help to carry each other's burdens; this is simply carrying out Christ's instructions. If anyone thinks he is too important to stoop to this, he really isn't worth anything and only fools himself.

Let everyone weigh up his contribution, to see whether he is doing enough. Then he can take pride in his own work, without making odious comparisons with what others are doing. For each must shoulder his own load of responsibility.

A person who is being taught to understand God's Word should give his teacher a share in the material things of life.

Don't be under any illusion – no-one can turn their nose up at God and get away with it. It is a universal law that a man must reap exactly what he has been sowing. If he cultivates his old self, he will harvest a character that has gone rotten. If he cultivates God's Spirit, that Spirit will produce life of a lasting quality.

So let us never get fed up with doing good. One day

there will be a grand harvest, if we don't give up. So whenever we get the chance, let's give as much help as we can to everybody, and especially to our immediate family of fellow-believers. Look what sprawling letters I use in my own handwriting!

It is those who are concerned about outward appearances and like to show off who are pressurising you into being circumcised. Their real object is to avoid the unpopularity associated with the cross of the Messiah. Even though they observe circumcision, they don't seem to bother about the rest of the Jewish law. They only want to get you circumcised so that they can brag about the number of converts to their ritual.

Never let me boast about anything or anybody – except the cross of Jesus the Messiah, our Lord. Through that execution I am dead to society and society is dead to me. Our standing in Christ is neither helped by being circumcised nor hindered by remaining uncircumcised. What really matters is being made into a new person inside. All who live by the simple principle will receive the undisturbed harmony and undeserved help of God, as the true Israel will.

From now on, let no-one interfere with my work again. I have the marks I want on my body; I am branded with scars gained in the service of Jesus.

May the generous love of Jesus, our divine Master and anointed Saviour, fill your inmost being, my brothers. So be it.

8

CANCER IN THE BODY
(Jude)

Introduction

Churches are more often and more easily destroyed from the inside than the outside.

This short, sharp letter from a younger brother of Jesus acts like a surgeon's knife to deal with a cancer spreading through the body of a church. Four stages of the disease are traced.

First, their **creed** is corrupted – with a sentimental view of God and a syncretistic view of Jesus.

Second, their **conduct** is corrupted – as it was with Israel in the wilderness, among the angels and in Sodom and Gomorrah.

Third, their **character** is corrupted – with Cain's anger, Balaam's avarice and Korah's ambition.

Fourth, their **conversation** is corrupted – by grumblers and fault-finders, boasters and flatterers.

They should have anticipated this danger; both prophets and apostles predicted it. They will have to deal with it by building themselves up in faith, hope and love – and by helping others in mental doubt, mortal danger or moral defilement.

God is able to keep them, if they keep themselves in his love.

This neglected epistle has so much to say to the modern church that I just had to put it into contemporary idiom.

Jude

This letter comes from Judas, Jude for short, one of the slaves bought by King Jesus and a brother of the James you well know.

It is addressed to those who have been called out of the world, who are now loved ones in the family of God their Father and who are being kept for presentation to King Jesus.

May you have more and more of the mercy, peace and love you have already experienced!

Loved ones, I was fully intending to correspond with you about the wonderful salvation we share, but found I had to write quite a different kind of letter. I must urge you to keep up the painful struggle for the preservation of the true faith, which was passed on to the early saints once and for all.

I have heard that certain persons, who shall be nameless, have sneaked in among you, godless men whose sentence of doom was pronounced long ago. They twist the free grace of God into an excuse for blatant immorality and they deny that King Jesus is our only master and Lord.

Now I want to remind you of some of those absolute truths which you already know perfectly well, particularly that God is not someone to be trifled with. You will recall that the Lord brought a whole nation safely out of Egypt but the next time he intervened they were all exterminated for not trusting him. Nor were his angels any more exempt than his people. When some of them deserted their rank and abandoned their proper station, he took them into custody and is keeping them permanently chained in the lowest and darkest dungeon until their trial on the great day of judgement. In the same way, the inhabitants of Sodom and Gomorrah, together with those from two neighbouring towns, glutted themselves with gross debauchery, craving for abnormal intercourse, just as the angels had done. The fate they suffered, in the fire that burned for ages, is a solemn warning to us all.

In spite of such examples in history, these people who have wormed their way into your fellowship pollute their own bodies in exactly the same manner, belittle divine authority and smear angels in glory. Yet even the chief of all angels, Michael, whose very name means: "godlike", did not dare to accuse Satan directly of blasphemy, when they were arguing about who owned the body of Moses; he was content to leave accusations to God himself and said simply, "The Lord rebuke you". But these men among you don't hesitate to malign whatever they don't understand; and the only things they do understand will prove their undoing in the end, for their knowledge of life comes only from their animal instincts, like brute beasts without any capacity for reason.

Woe betide them! They have gone down the same road as Cain. They have rushed headlong into the same mistake as Balaam – and for the same motive, money. They come to the same end as Korah did in his rebellion.

These people have the cheek to eat with you at your fellowship meals of love, though they are only looking for pasture for themselves. Like submerged rocks, they could wreck everything! They are like clouds, driven past so hard by the wind that they give no rain. They are like uprooted trees in the autumn, with neither leaves nor fruit, doubly dead. They are like wild waves of the sea, stirring up the filthy foam of their own odious disgrace. They are like shooting stars, falling out of orbit, destined to disappear down a "black hole" for ever.

Enoch, who lived only seven generations after the first man, Adam, saw all this coming. He was referring to these very people when he made his prophetic announcement: "Look out! The Lord has arrived with ten thousand of his angels to put all human beings on trial and convict all godless people of all godless deeds they have committed in their godless lives and of the hard things these godless sinners have spoken against him".

These people are discontented grumblers, always complaining and finding fault. Their mouths are full of big talk about themselves, but they are not above flattering others when it is to their advantage.

Now, loved ones, you should have remembered what the apostles of our Lord Jesus Christ said would happen. They predicted that, "in the final age there are bound to be those who pour scorn on godliness, whose lives will only be governed by their own godless cravings". People like this can only create divisions among you, since they only have their natural instincts to go by and lack the guidance of the Spirit.

As for you, loved ones, be sure to go on building yourselves up on the solid foundation of your most holy faith, praying in the way the Spirit gives you. Stay in love with God, waiting patiently for the time when our Lord Jesus Christ in his sheer mercy will bring you into immortal living.

As regards the others, here is my advice. To those who are still wavering be especially kind and gentle. Those who have already been led into error must be snatched from the fire before they are badly burned. Those who have been thoroughly contaminated should be treated better than they deserve, though you must never lose a healthy fear of being infected yourself, even by their stained underwear.

Let's just praise the one person who is able to keep you from stumbling and to make you stand upright in his glorious presence, without any imperfection but with great jubilation, the only God there is and he's our Saviour too, through Jesus Christ our Lord – for to him alone belongs all glory, all majesty, all power and all authority – before history began, now in this present time and for all ages to come. Absolutely true!